MW01600355

For Always

Shannon O'Connor

ISBN: 9781720211297

Independently Published

Edited by Cheyenne Raine

Shannon O'Connor

Also by Shannon O'Connor

For Always

"You're braver than you believe,
stronger than you seem,
and smarter than you think"
-Christopher Robin to
Winnie The Pooh

Shannon O'Connor

Acknowledgments

To the girl who broke my heart and the guy who broke my trust. Thank you for the inspiration and the memories.

A lot has changed in the years since this collection was first published. In many ways I am not the same person who wrote these poems or feel these words. This second edition adds some poems with growth and a different outlook on things.

Shannon O'Connor

For Always

For Katie

Shannon O'Connor

The Lightning Strikes:
Part I

Shannon O'Connor

Lightning

It's intense
hitting you hard all at once
God she's beautiful
you say it out loud
she blushes.

You think you've never seen anything so beautiful
her face is a work of art
eyes you get lost in
a jaw so sharp it could cut glass
and a mouth that pulls me in.

Her smile is small
the world had gotten to her.
Her kisses were delicate,
soft and slow,
best of all were the sounds she made,

her laugh was contagious
her sobs broke my heart
Her moans sent chills down my spine
and her voice could calm storms
like the ones in my head.

She came out of nowhere,
a siren in the sea
like Daisy in the green light
something rare,
like getting struck by lighting.

Fools

They say only fools fall in love
then I must be crazy
because I'm not just in love
I'm head over heels
falling on my face in love with you.

It wasn't planned
but since the day I met you
I've been tripping over pebbles
getting paper cuts writing you love poems.

I wanted you to love me too
so I kissed you
but I got caught in your eyes
and bumped your nose too.

But that was only the start
I've been falling for years
now you've finally caught me
and said you loved me too.

Sing
Our song,
the one on the radio
that everyone knew
always reminded me of you.

You would sing
loudly and off key
but would always sound
the sweetest to me.

Fireworks

Maybe I miss you
and the way things used to be
throwing your head back with laughter
being yourself with me.

I remember that day
with our faces
just inches away
and no one would know.

What if I leaned
and our lips would touch
in that perfect way
where fireworks would burn.

Three Simple Words

Three simple words
could make everything,
so complicated
it could make or break a relationship
and be the reason to leave or stay.

Three simple words
which I've said to you
seem to mean nothing
while you say those words,
to someone else.

Three simple words
cannot even begin to describe
how I feel.
They don't mean enough
or say exactly what I mean.

I want the world for you
and for you to see how amazing you are,
how much you mean to me
and how much you mean,
to everyone else.

You are my world
you make me smile
and laugh
and I will always
want to be with you.

I wish you saw me
in a new light
and I could hear those
three simple words:
'I love you'

Into The Cold

Her lips are blue
shivering from the cold
she says the line
and you take her hand.

Her hand warms up
and you go to let go
but instead she puts a hand on your cheek
causing you to blush.

your cheeks turn red
and she gets closer
not saying a word
but you know she feels what you do.

All those months of doubt
melts into the snow
as she comes closer
face to face.

You push her bangs behind her ear,
and lean in
your lips are inches apart
and you can smell her peppermint gum

your lips touch
and for once
you can't breathe
you're melting into a puddle,

because she melted your heart
and everything just
felt right
and okay.

Storms
You made life breathable again
you took my hand
and calmed the storms in my head
because you had a tornado in yours too.

Gatsby's Eyes

It's in the eyes
the way you can tell
how someone
truly feels.

She would smile
and laugh
and was happy
but her eyes were telling another story.

She had feelings
but she wasn't in love
forcing herself to lie
that love and lust were the same.

Temptation

Her eyes played tricks
never knowing quite what she was thinking
she touched my arm
and blushed
and stumbled.

She lusted me,
I could tell by the contact
the way she got nervous around me
and the way she lost her words.

But was a simple kiss worth it?
no, a kiss is never just a kiss
especially when you're taken
and the one you love isn't her.

I couldn't
I shouldn't
but damn
I'm tempted.

Her smile,
God her laugh
it sounded like angels singing
I could hear it forever.

But no,
I was taken
and flirting is just flirting
and I can't read into a thing.

Because there's another girl I love
another girl I'm going to marry
and start a family with
and she's just my destruction.
or so I thought.

Love I
Fresh and pure
exciting and new
young love
this time
I fell in love with myself
and I couldn't imagine looking back.

Love II
Getting married
having kids
buying a house
a future.
That's all I've ever wanted
but one day
you said you wanted it too
and I knew then,
I no longer wanted it with you.

Pizza Girl

We sat on the hood of your car
eating pizza
from the second shop we visited
wanting to compare our favorites.

You were impressed with mine,
eating almost the whole slice
passing me bites
in-between the laughter.

I'd pause forever in that moment;
just you and me
laughing and smiling
being free.

I hadn't checked my phone in hours
it was on silent
knowing she'd call,
but I didn't want any interruptions.

I wanted you and I
and that moment,
looking at the stars
getting lost on a drive.

I didn't think about anything else
when we were together,
there was no pressure
no expectations with you.

You lived in the moment
and I
for once
was living there with you.

You got me into trouble,
I hadn't expected you
or to fall as hard as I did
but you were different.

You didn't fit into a box
no stereotypes;
you were surprises
and living without a care.

You were everything I needed,
but was too afraid to go after.
My one regret
now that it's too late.

Feeling Alive

We laughed about nothing
driving in the night
talking about the world
getting lost in our small town.

My head was heavy
constantly struggling,
but being with you
took that away.

No trouble,
no planning,
just going
and looking back later.

You were a breath of fresh air
letting me be free
joining you on the adventure
you called life.

You had your own demons
but they never took your smile,
never took your free spirit,
and your taste for living.

You made me feel
in a time
where I was numb.

It Was Like I Was Drowning

You were like coming up for air,
I couldn't breathe
when I was with her.
I could barely speak
or smile,
or be me.

But with you,
I finally caught my breath.
I could be myself
and for some reason,
that's when you liked me best.

So I took off my mask,
and broke down my walls,
giving you a chance to break my heart;
something you've done before.

But this time you didn't,
You fell harder than I did
and you picked up every piece
that she broke before you.

You had a few broken pieces too,
and maybe that's why we worked.
We both knew what it was like
to fall in love with the wrong girl.

For Always

He had the smirk
aka
my weakness,
my **kryptonite**.

Flirting
was his second nature
and breaking hearts
was first.

He was exactly my type,
the type
I should
stay away from

He was a smooth talker
used to getting what he wants
and I wanted to challenge that
but I was putty in his hands.

Keeping me on my toes
with 100 questions
while keeping himself
a mystery.

Rebound
It's fresh,
exciting
you're blushing
laughing to yourself
trying not to seem too eager
worrying about the little things
wondering how soon
is too soon.

Big Deal

You let me put my guard down
I could laugh
and be myself
I wasn't self conscious.

You were fantastic
in case you were wondering;
I often describe you
as the best.

I hope you won't be embarrassed by this
it's not at all
a love poem
but more of a thank you.

You helped me
and let me be me
in a time of need
so thank you

For letting me tease you
In more way than one,
leaving my mark on you
and being kind of a big deal.

Struck

5 years down the road
our coffee shop
I'm on my way to work,
hot chocolate in hand
I'm running late as usual

I'm not looking where I'm going-
SHIT
hot chocolate all over my dress
and thats when I hear it
the laugh that changed my life

I glance up surprised
'you always were clumsy' she chuckled
years of memories come floating back
a familiar sense of home
like nothing had changed

I struggled not to look like a fool
but its too late for that
this isn't the worst she's seen me
we always said we'd do this
true believers of fate.

For Always

The Storm:
Part II

The First Time

You put your hand on my leg,
looking at me expectantly.
I was afraid,
and I think you sensed my fear.
I hated feeling inferior
so I didn't say a word as you whispered in my ear.

You told me to kiss you first
I took a deep breath and leaned in,
ignoring every gut feeling telling me to run.
I tried to get more into it as I got on top
I mean, wasn't losing your virginity supposed to be
fun?

But I ignored my fears
and everything inside me telling me no
as I let you take off my dress.
You worked quickly,
undressing me piece by piece.

I ignored it when you kissed me
and I thought of her.
I ignored it when the butterflies turned into knots
and each touch left a bruise.
I let you touch me,
making me feel more naked than I was.

You made me feel exposed.
I lost my voice when I was with you.
I could never say a word
even though it hurt.
Everything hurt when I was with you.

I guess I was just used to you hurting me
so why should sex be any different?
But as you touched me,
I let my mind drift.

I went to my happy place,
I pretended what you did was good
I let you use me in a new way that day.
And I'll forever regret,
losing my virginity to a girl I thought I loved.

He had to focus on the road,
on not crashing the car.
It gave me control
the one time
he couldn't overpower me
or stop me
or really even speak.
-The art of giving road head

I Know You
It's 2am
you can't sleep
you're worried about everything
your head is going crazy
weeks left
worried about the future
trying to live in the moment
that isn't you.
Trying to change
for her
losing yourself
but at least
you're not alone,
except at night
when she's not there
and the voices are back
telling you everything
you fear most.

The Little Mermaid
When I was with you
I lost me.
I followed your lead,
letting you take parts of me, too.

My voice was the first to go,
I think you took it one day,
Like Ursula
And locked it in a shell.

I couldn't speak
and I let you do what you pleased.
As long as you were happy,
who cared about me?

Next was my happiness,
you took that day by day
week by week,
until there was nothing left.

You took my smile,
you took my laugh,
and you made me question
if I was even allowed to be happy.

When I was with you,
I couldn't breathe.
I questioned every action
and worried you'd get upset

I never realized
I was walking around
living in fear,
of the girl I thought I loved.

Heart
You were fucking other girls
and I felt guilty when a girl kissed my cheek.

The Other Woman
I lied,
I knew about you,
who you were
and all that you two had.

I convinced myself
you were all the things he said,
you didn't make him happy
and you were crazy.

I let him play the victim
while letting him
paint a scarlet 'A'
on my chest.

I chose to focus
on the way he made me feel,
special, loved,
and protected.

I pushed you out of my mind,
as he kissed my neck,
tore off my clothes,
and made me forget my name.

I pretended that feeling in my stomach,
the knots of guilt
was nothing,
as I laid next to him in bed.

But as it became more than that,
more than a one time thing
and more than friends
it was harder to forget about you.

I fell in love
and his heart opened up,
I tried not to think of you
as I asked him to choose me.

He agreed to my selfish request,
ending things with you
which should have calmed my stomach,
yet I just felt worse.

Things with us changed,
he held me differently,
there were emotions in his kiss,
love in his touch.

I thought about you less
but wondered
if he made you feel this way
and I tried not to think about how long it would last.

The Truth I
She doesn't mean anything.
She's just a friend.
I don't think of her in that way.
Don't you trust me?

The Truth II

I beg
just be honest with me
tell me the truth
I already know
but she insisted on lying

It's nothing.
Theres no one else.
You're crazy,
don't you trust me?

When she said those words
I knew it was over
if you have to ask,
the trust is already gone.

For Always

How do you define cheating?
There's the obvious,
but what about before that?

Is it cheating when she makes your heart flutter?
What about when your hands touch
and you feel a spark?
When she hugs you
and the smell of her perfume
stays with you all day.

What about when you go for a drive
and she tries to kiss you?
You say no but your heart is screaming yes.
Is it only cheating when your lips touch?

When a kiss becomes more
and you've forgotten about anyone else.
What makes a cheater?

You can't control feelings
yet if I knew how she made you feel
while you were still mine
I'd feel like that was cheating,
so where's the line?

Good Enough
You held my hand
and said you'd never go.
You let me in
and said it'd be different.

I believed you,
and let my walls down
pushing you away
because that's what I do.

I was scared
but you said you'd never go
I believed you
and here I am alone.

Left to pick up
the pieces you left,
the ones you used
and decided weren't good enough.

Needy

Don't do it
she isn't worth it
the voices taunt me
I can't be that girl.

I don't need to talk every minute of the day
I don't need to know where you are
but it'd put my mind at ease
calm the voices.

I text again,
no response
34 minutes now
but who's really counting?

You're being needy
she can do better
36 minutes
my phone lights up.

Target is having a sale
I turn on the sound
knowing fully that won't make the waiting easier
40 minutes.

God, I'm needy
I hate myself for this
but every night here I am
counting the fucking minutes.

43 now
It's late
But we promised to talk
So I wait up,

I'm about to give up
48 minutes
Ding! Ding! Ding!
I held my phone like a winning lottery ticket.

Gone.
Click.
No new posts.
Refresh.
No new posts.

I tell myself to
calm down
of course that only makes it worse

My breath quickens
as my heart races
I'm a wreck
worrying about you

What the hell should I be doing?
3 years and it's over in a text
of course I'm going to check in
there's someone else

Isn't there always?
I'm driving myself crazy
but I'm not wrong
refresh.

There it is.
3 days later.
3 years gone.
In a matter of 3 seconds.

Call Me
I don't call
not because
I don't miss you
because
I don't think
I could handle it
if you don't pick up.

Real Talk
Chained to my phone
waiting for your calls
your text
hoping it'll make everything okay
unable to move
and live
in fear of missing you
worried we won't be the same
wondering if this is how love should be.

I hate social media
Posting photos of your stupid food
your location
every minute of the damn day
telling strangers your feelings
commenting on everything
checking in on exes,
wondering what they're up to
being too weak to pick up the phone
seeing that stupid purple heart
and wanting emojis to go extinct
seeing playlists of the same songs
you called 'ours'
the internet is a scary place
knowledge is power
and I don't want any of it.

Feelings Fade
You can fuck her
until you feel nothing
until you fall in love
until you convince yourself it's okay
until you believe you're happy.
But that orgasm will wear off
and you'll have her
in your bed
wishing it was me.
Wondering how it got this bad
wishing things were different
when it's all too late.
So fuck her
until you forget me
but I know you think of me
and when she's not good enough
your feelings will still be there
and I won't be.

I'm Okay
People keep asking if I'm okay
I lie to make them happy
of course I'm not okay.

They tell me what you're up to
like I would want to know,
they lie
say you look unhappy
that it will never last

They tell me about her too,
tell me what I want to hear
tearing her down in the process

If I say I'm okay,
will you let me move on?

Real

If our love had been real
I would've waited.
If there was potential
I would've waited.

I waited a year for you to be mine
fought like hell but by then
I should've realized
you were never mine.

I could've said no
to the blonde with the sun kissed tan
who melted my heart
and saved others on the daily.

I could've said no
to the flirt
who couldn't be faithful
and keep her hands off me.

I could've said no
to the drives home from the brunette
with the laugh and smile
that made my day.

I should've said no
to the guy
with the power
and the smirk that sent me chills.

For the times I should've said no
what about all the times you said yes
for all the girls whose names I don't know
and all the ones I do.

For all the fights
all the lies
and all the doubts
and the times you called me crazy.

But in reality
if there was ever a chance
for a real us
anyone else
wouldn't have been a choice.

Her
You were in my dreams again
rather I should say nightmares.
Her hands were all over you
in the ways mine used to be

Each time
I tried looking away
my mind would hit replay

Each touch felt like knives
dragged into my heart.
That should be me
I tried to scream

No sound escaped my lips
I stayed frozen,
unable to move
each kiss killing me more than the last.

Desperate

She hung to my every word
looking for a hidden meaning
She stuck to my side like glue
not wanting to let me go
it should have been sweet
but why did I feel trapped?

I invited her
but it's not like I had a choice
What were my options?
Bring her
or leave her
and have to hear about it all year.

So I invited her
expected it to be casual
she didn't know what that word meant.
She was like a lion
ready to pounce
on anyone that threatened her mate.

But I wasn't her mate
and she couldn't handle that,
she said she understood
wanted me to roam free
yet stayed on me like a leech
sucking the life right out of me.

For Always

I see red
everywhere I go.
Your stupid red car
that you drive too fast.

I wonder if you still snap and drive
I wonder if it worries her too
and she tells you to slow down
but I doubt she cares.

She's not in your car for good
she's temporary,
but I'm
sitting passenger to your life now.

Watching you and her
pass me by,
does she know
what happened in that car?

How we made love in the back seat?
and in the front?
the tears we cried
the fights we shared.

Does she feel that?
When the speedometer ticks to 85
I would clench my jaw
begging you to slow down.

What about the fights?
The bad one
the one about that stupid button
and all the ones in between.

The goodbye kisses
the hello kisses
at 6am when you drove me to work
and you were the only thing to make me smile.

How about that reminder on the mirror?
The green light
the hope for us
is it still there?
-Or Did You Replace That, Too?

Fear

Why wasn't I enough?
Was I needy?
I cried too much?
I cared too much?

Because I'd love to know
why 3 years
seemed to mean nothing
but was my entire life.

We fought,
but only when we were apart
and it was always the same thing;
I miss you and come home to me.

We couldn't stay apart
we loved each other too much
the connection was too deep
an electric feeling every time we touched.

But that wasn't enough
she got scared
the future was unknown
and this was the only thing she could control.

Home

I kept your T-shirt
the yellow cotton one
with the cliche logo
that was your favorite.

It smelled like you
and made me feel at home
I could close my eyes
and your arms were wrapped around me.

You told me not to lose it
you were anxious with me borrowing it
but it was special so I kept it safe
I only wish you did the same with my heart.

You held that close
until you didn't want it anymore
and you threw it away
like a ratty T-shirt.

So when it came time
to give back your things
I had to keep your favorite T-shirt
that smelled like you.

Because that's all I had left;
the memories and laughs
and I couldn't bear to see
her get the shirt, too
after all,
she already got you.

Promise

I found my ring today
I hadn't seen it in weeks
forgotten about its existence
but there it was
reminding me
what it once meant
what it once symbolized
all that hope
love
and promises
that ring had a lot of pressure.
I thought about what to do with it
I couldn't bring myself to throw it away
I couldn't give it back
and I wondered
what you did with yours.
We gave our stuff back;
I got my clothes
and photos
and some letters,
but you kept a lot of letters
and the ring wasn't there.
Did you throw it away?
I like to think that you still have it
locked somewhere
she won't find it.

That you kept
some reminder of me.
I put my ring in my jewelry box
saving it for the future
knowing it'll be a story to tell
to a kid who isn't yours.
I'll tell them
about all it represented
and the girl it was from
knowing you're someone
I won't forget.

Replaceable
You promised you wouldn't replace me
but I was boarding the plane home
and she was already moving in
You said she didn't mean anything
yet she was saying 'I love you'
The hardest part is realizing
how little I meant to you
How easily replaceable I was.

I'm Just Curious
You said
'she meant nothing'
and
'you didn't want her'
you told me
everything to keep me,
I have the texts.
were you lying to me?
Or
are you still lying to her?

Denial

I wonder if you talk about me
if you told her about me
about how we were together,
probably not.

You hate talking about the past
you live in the present
and focus on the future
the past is full of regrets to you.

I wonder if she knows about me,
about the plans for the future we had;
our tower by the ocean
your dogs and our kids.

Does she know how I felt?
The years I fought to be with you
the letters I wrote you
the photos and memories we had.

I'm sure she knows the bad;
the way I hated your planning
the fights we had
and the way we treated each other at the end.

But did you tell her about the good?
the bridge in central park
the stage and bumping noses
the smile you gave me the last time I saw you.

Does she know it was real,
the love we shared,
the future we had planned
or did you replace that too?

For Always

You changed my wiring;
the way I think.
I can't eat
I can't sleep
I can't fuck without feelings
I can't think about anyone else
you changed me.
Making me feel something inside
I can't look at anyone else
I can't kiss her
I can't feel something for him
I can't even think about sex
it all feels like cheating.
Why do I feel like
I'm doing something wrong?
When you're in bed with her,
telling her the same things
you told me.
**-You changed me
and I want the old me back**

No Excuses
Someone like her doesn't change,
she won't change her ways
she showed her true colors
you can't ignore it.
No matter
how beautiful
how many good memories
how she made you feel
it doesn't change what she did
the choices she made
and you can't make excuses
for someone
who excused your feelings.

See-Saw

She was a coward
pathetic and afraid
of anything real
that had the power to hurt her.

She claimed to be practical
that's why life needed a plan,
she couldn't bear the thought
of living in the unknown.

That's what broke us
my spontaneity and living in the unknown,
fun and impractical,
late, head stuck in the clouds.

Total opposites,
we should have balanced out
but the see-saw tipped
in one direction,

eventually making her leave
needing the stability
only someone on the ground
could give her.

Why'd You Leave?
I can't imagine doing this again;
getting to know someone
finding them cute
falling for them
them falling for me
falling in love
kissing
holding hands
touching
I feel physically ill
trying to imagine
being with anyone else.

My Favorite State
I don't hate you
some say I should
some wonder how I don't
in reality I pity you.

You claim to be a feminist
an activist for Women's rights
yet take down other women
for personal gain.

I understand you
she's perfect,
how could you not fall in love
right?

But in the middle
of her crying her side to you
claiming to be the victim
did you stop and look?

You ignored the facts
twisted your grip on her
and hoped she'd fall
as hard as you did for her.

Thats why I pity you
because girls who are so insecure
that they need to steal
from other girls
need to be loved.

So take her
enjoy the prize you believe you're getting
but in the end
shell screw you over, too.

The only difference is,
you'll be left with no love for yourself-
I knew when to walk away
and know when
to pity an insecure girl.

Holding On
You did this
took my heart
twisting it around your talons
making me feel broken
letting the voice in my head take over
making me feel like a bother
isolating me
leaving me without friends
while you were always out
leaving me home
worried.
You always had one foot out the door,
never being all in
having a back up
and new options
at your beck and call,
making me push to keep you
scared I'd lose you.
Not knowing
that if you have to fight
to keep someone
they were already gone.

Opposites

I crave closeness,
but when you show me affection I run.

I crave security,
but when you talk about the future I get
scared.

I want honesty,
but I'm afraid to be honest with you.

I don't want to feel trapped,
yet I make you feel suffocated.

It's not you
She'll change you;
one day you're happy
both experiencing life
happy to be in love
with someone who just gets you.

Then it changes
she's dark
and non responsive
her heart is closed
and you're wondering where you went wrong.

You'll spend weeks
and months
trying to get back what you had,
that first feeling
all that happiness and love.

But it won't come back,
you can spend forever
trying to get that girl back
but she's gone
and it'll break you.

You'll be up
wondering what went wrong
constantly trying to fix things
working on it
doing everything right.

But she's gone
and now you've lost yourself too.
Gone is the person you were
and you wonder how you got there,
so know that it's not you.

She did this before you
and she'll do it after you.
She breaks people
because of how broken
she is inside.

When you finally realize
you've had enough,
and you step back,
you'll see it from my side
knowing where you went wrong
was falling in love
with a broken girl.

Temporary

A song came on the radio today
you'd love it
it's exactly your taste
and the lyrics were great.

I looked it up
and almost sent it to you
then I remembered
we're on different paths.

It wasn't you, it was me
the timing just wasn't right
and all those other cliches
you tried to give me as an excuse.

Losing a best friend
might be worse than losing a love.
You're alone again
forced to start over with a sense of lost balance.

Everything seems different
you question why people get close
and before long
you've isolated yourself from the world.

Days go by with no communication
you start to feel empty
and that's when you fill the void
at least temporarily.

Like a Book
You were angry
when he came into my life,
threatened by him
scared he'd take me.

People aren't possessions
he couldn't take me,
unless I wanted to go
but you knew I did.

You never gave me a reason to stay,
but you told me all the reasons to go
pushing me into his arms,
getting upset at each touch.

He read me
like you never could,
taking the time to understand me
instead of pushing me away.

You were threatened
not because he wanted me,
but threatened I would go
and not look back.

500 Miles

Was I not good enough?
I didn't fit into your image
we were from two different worlds
but you were my best friend,
right?

You hated me at first
I guess I never let that go
I mean who really could?
knowing your best friend never wanted you around
it fucks with you.

We took drives that summer
no destination,
just blasting music and singing off key
sometimes turning it down to talk.

The moments where we didn't have anything to say
the moments where we needed to explain
everything,
When I couldn't get the words out
but you just knew
I miss that most.

500 miles didn't seem that far until you left
you said we'd keep in touch
we wouldn't be a statistic.
I believed it,
and at first I think you meant it, too.

Then you came back
and you were different.
You weren't my best friend anymore
college had changed you
made you hard.

You held back,
I couldn't talk to you anymore
I was in the way,
a bother
and my problems were nothing to yours.

I ignored it at first
you had gone through a lot
I should be understanding
so I sucked it up
took the punches and kept quiet.

But I became a ticking bomb,
you were different
and being around you made me different,
it changed me, too
and I had to stand up for myself.

So maybe this was out of nowhere to you
but for me,
this was months
of feeling like nothing
and a backup friend to you.

People say growing apart is normal
high school friendships don't last,
not in the real world.
I guess what's most surprising is
you said you wouldn't and you fucking did.

Mint To Be

I didn't imagine it would end this way
your heart intertwined
with someone else
while I'm still in your head.

And yet here we are,
ending things
prematurely.

Meeting to say goodbye
with our hearts not in it
begging to give it one last try
but scared to get hurt again.

I want to say
how much I'll always care
how I'll miss your smile
and the way you say my name.

Love you
I can't choke out the words
afraid you won't say it
knowing that would break me.

Let me go,
but don't forget me
the good and the bad.
Even after all this time,
I know what you're thinking
so I'll say it out loud
"I love you, too".

Reflection
I'm sorry
I don't think I ever said it
I was too proud
and too stubborn
to admit I was wrong.

I'm sorry
maybe if I would've said that more
and admitted when you were right
there'd still be a chance
and there's still be an us.

I'm sorry,
if I meant it back then
it could've changed everything
but then I wouldn't have learned
to stand on my own.

If I said it back then
you wouldn't have learned
to stand up for yourself
to be brave
and speak your mind.

So I wonder now
how much
those two words
could have changed everything
I'm sorry.

Mustang

I want that night back,
you know the one
it was my favorite night,
because it was the one
where I realized
I fell in love with you.
It was late December,
we were in the back of your car
half naked,
I was laying in your lap,
running my hands through your beard
and you were playing with my hair.
The radio was low
the heat was on high
I used your shirt as a blanket
not wanting to get dressed
not wanting to end our night.
You told me about your heart
how broken it was,
we both cried that night
knowing our time was limited.
You held me,
told me I was beautiful
and wiped my tears
you kissed my head
and I felt safe
not knowing how badly
this would turn out.

I'm sorry I loved him
that's what you want me to say right?
You want to blame him
I fell in love with someone else
and that's what broke us?
We were broken
long before he came along.
I fell in love with him
because I no longer loved you
in a way that was healthy.
I needed a way out
a way to feel alive again
after you took everything from me.
So I gave my heart to him
and he shattered it
into a million pieces
leaving you to be right
(for once)
and needing comfort
I ran back to you
to put me back together.
Not realizing
you were the one
to break me first.
-I'm not sorry

Heartbeat

One minute I was yelling
screaming at you to listen
the next minute
I couldn't breathe
my words were gone
I was shaking
he panicked
she came to my rescue
like she always did.
He stood there stunned
I focused on breathing
her voice calmed me
they went blurry
she panicked,
gave me water
and I was back to normal.
She gave me her jacket
a true gentle-woman
Shivering I told her to go
walk away
let me handle this
why the hell did she listen to me?

Irony

It was over back then
but you couldn't see it
your heart was confused
stuck in an alternate future.

I didn't want to go
so I tried to help you understand
but I fell back in love
and wished for a second chance.

By then you understood
you moved on with someone else
leaving me heartbroken
when I was the one who wanted to leave.

No?
We live in a society
where saying no
doesn't mean no.
When turning someone down
you have to hope
for a good reaction
and be prepared
for a bad reaction.

My Storm

His smirk was a drug
along with his words
they could cut like knives
or pull me down deeper.

His eyes played games
a strong facade kept everyone out
convinced that was for the best
even though it was the loneliest.

He was hard on himself
but to others he was the one they could hate,
in hopes that no one would miss him.

He had pain in his heart
it had been broken too many times
which left him breaking others
doing the breaking was less painful for him.

He was reckless
and he drank too much,
but drinking numbed his pain
and being numb was better than dealing with the
hurt.

He had arms that when wrapped around you,
could make you feel safe
his heart beat fast and he was warm
he made you comfortable.
He was honest,
his words could make you forget everything
or change entirely how you feel.

For Always

Head in the Clouds:
Part III

For Always

It became the norm;
it didn't change overnight
but slowly and surely,
it became a habit.

A night out drinking
became drinking in alone
and a twisted tea
turned into half a bottle of vodka.

No one noticed how bad it got,
that alcohol was missing
and I was constantly hungover
healing that with more alcohol.

I woke up
not able to handle my thoughts
not wanting to see the chaos
I created called my life.

Going out to drink with friends
became a weekly tradition
but drinking alone
became a nightly tradition.

Sneaking juice and rum
or Jack and Coke
whatever I could get my hands on really
just to calm my head.

To numb the thoughts
and chaos
that I made
to shut out the world.

A few nights out
with excuses of parties
became mixed

with nights alone in my room.

Doing shots
chugging mixed drinks
praying I wouldn't get sick
but knowing I would.

Just for those few hours
of nothing,
the numbness
of shutting my brain off.

Blacking out was rare
so I was never ready when it happened
always wondering
what happened in those hours lost.

Not knowing how to stop
becoming irritable without it
seeing the signs of addiction
not recognizing myself in the mirror.

Knowing I had to stop
and wanting to stop
were two different things
until she said those horrible words.

I cleaned up my act
pouring the hidden bottles down the sink
those words working better
than cold water to the face.

-You're turning into your father

Vodka Thoughts I

I used to reach for you,
now I reach for a bottle.
A hangover
feels better than you.

Vodka Thoughts II
It's hard to tell
whether feeling everything
or feeling nothing
is better.

Hit It
She says hit it,
it'll make you feel better.
Some smoke blows in my face
I wonder how I got here.

She holds out the joint
I hesitate
She laughs in my face,
smoke blows right out
and I cough a storm.

How did I get here?
To a place with no say
A place where I don't feel safe.

Sippin'

There's something familiar
about the fuzziness
the way it makes my head quiet
and my body feel warm.
There's comfort in the bubbles
as they head to my stomach
making my lips tingle
and the effects kick in.
Chugging
and sipping
taking turns between
feeling the rush
and enjoying the buzz.

Drink Up

There are repercussions
for each drop you pour
each sip you take
and each shot you swallow.

A tipsy hello
a drunk text
a drunken kiss
going home with someone else.

Each day you drink,
another night alone
another day of numbing the pain
takes a toll.

You mumble "I'm fine"
stumbling out of the bar
blacking out on the way home
not sure if you want to wake up the next
morning.

Morning After

I chug a bottle of water
Set the tylenol on the nightstand
Hope tomorrow's headache won't be as bad
But it always is.

Lost In Smoke

Smokey rooms,
faded people
faded thoughts
take a sip
forget it tonight.

You can tell the drunk from the sober
we each take a sip,
drowning the sorrows
trying too hard
and forgetting everything tonight.

There's an agenda;
looks like you're having a good time,
find someone to love
or find someone to make you forget.

Some come for the thrill
some come for the alcohol
and mostly,
people come to be someone else for a night.

Girls squeezed into too tight crop tops
guys playing beer pong to impress
the thumping music prevents talking
unless you lean in.

Alcohol and hormones mix
talking becomes kissing
kissing becomes touching
and soon you're lost in a world of senses.

The End

The tears are pouring down my face
my lips are dry
and my head is pounding.
I have the chills
and I can't breathe
I feel suffocated by my own thoughts.

I know what would ease the pressure.
I know what could make me feel better.

But I couldn't dare
because I'm staying alive
to make everyone else happy.
I'm suffering through each day
because it's what everyone says is best.

I can't handle her sobs over my casket
thinking it was her fault.

So I wake up each day,
and I take a breath
and I try to beat what the day gives me.
Even though,
it might kill me.

Fake It

I just want your arms around me
telling me it's okay,
but your mind is on her
so I'm holding the blade
wondering if it's worth it anymore
wondering if there's even a point
wondering if there ever was.

What was the point of falling in love?
What was the point to anything?
I'm sitting on the bathroom floor crying to
myself because you're gone.
And wondering
if you were ever really here.

I worry that it's me.
It's always been me.

I lie and hide what I mean
I ignore the burning sensation each time I
lie
and choke out an "I'm fine"
no one really notices.

They say I should've been an actress
but I hate the stage.
I'm scared of rejection,
I'd love to be up there
soaking up the attention
but God knows I could never handle the
truth.

It's so much easier to hide behind a mask
or on the wings,
no one notices you there.
It's easier blending in
pretending I don't exist.

For Always

The Rain:
Part IV

All Of Me

I can no longer say the song is true
I no longer love "All of you"
not that you ever loved any of me,
of course.

I am so close
to almost being free,
to letting go of you
once and for all.

When I'm with her
I no longer think of you.
I'm me with her,
someone I never got to be with you.

Her smile makes the world stop
and I have to catch my breath.
When she bites her lip
and smirks at me.

I look at you,
and all I want to do is finally be free,
because "All of Me"
no longer loves all of you.

I tried to ignore it
I had asked for a sign;
this is not what I meant.
Don't send me back down that hole
Don't send me those signs.
That door was shut,
locked,
bolted,
all the windows are shatter proof,
every mouse hole closed.
There is no way back in,
please don't send me those signs.
-He was wearing lighting bolts

Growth

I walk outside
heart full of anger and determination
hands full of her clothes and letters,
then I see her

she looks up
catches me walking closer
her face lights up
like a kid on Christmas morning.

I'm imminently struck
buckets of feelings come pouring back
and a breath of relief calms my nerves
she loves me.

I push those feelings down
and let the pain resurface
ignore the urge to kiss her
ignore the urge to be home again.

We fight,
I remember why I'm here.
This is goodbye
this is closure.

The more we talk
the more we have to remind ourselves of
that
we picked up where we left off
I knew her better than anyone.

"Do you still love me?" I manage to choke
out
"Of course I do."
"I love you, too," I say holding back tears
but that doesn't fix everything.

Just because two people love each other
doesn't mean they should be together
sometimes people change
and love isn't enough.

Time

A year ago,
I gave you something I can't take back
something I often wish I could.

A year ago,
I was kissing your neck
and thinking of someone else as I faked the
pleasure.

A year ago,
I gave you a part of me that one of us can
take back
a part that changed us forever.

A year ago,
you touched my skin,
and made me feel naked.

Now, you touch someone else's skin
with no memory of me
forgetting all the things you once said.

Now, I found someone else
someone who's arms are my home
and their touch fills me with electricity.

Someone who loves me
and who never makes me feel naked
instead makes me feel beautiful
no matter what.

Change of Perspective

Change doesn't happen overnight
it doesn't happen at 3pm
when you're laughing with a friend
assuring her you're okay,

change doesn't happen at 5am
when you can't sleep
and she's on your mind
wondering where you went wrong.

Change is gradual
it sneaks up on you
when it's 6 months later
and she pops up as a recommended friend.

It's when you run into her in public
and you smile and mean it
it's when you can't sleep
and she's no longer the one you call.

Fixed Up
Her heart had tears
and scars
and was barely together
when we met.

I spent time
learning to sew
patch the tears
and cover the scars with kisses.

Trust was earned over time
each secret kept in a vault
learning something new everyday
and learning that's how you love someone.

It's not the look
the way they smile and you melt
the beautiful hazel eyes that look at you full
of love
it's the way you learn to love the other.

Time and patience
learning each and every secret and fear
that's how the heart truly loves
and with love
she was healed.

But that's when she decided
she didn't need me anymore
I had spent my time healing
and loving every inch.

But that's when she found out
she didn't need me
she didn't want me
and there was someone better.

But would they love you like I did?
Kiss every scar?
Turn on the light at night?
Hold you when you don't know how to say
you're sad?

She won't know you like I did
she won't make you feel the way I did
an electric, lighting feeling
you took for granted.

One

I cant help but wonder
how much
one choice,
one change,
one encounter,
one word,
one hello,
one goodbye,
one person,
one breath,
can truly affect
your life.

I Chose Wrong

If I could go back
hit rewind on the clock
I'd choose her
over you
every damn time.

Love;
drunk texting your best friend at 3am
your puppy licking your face
going for midnight drives
singing at the top of your lungs
driving with the windows down in the
summer
eating pizza that's too hot and burning your
mouth
laughing with your best friend
-Love isn't always romantic

Choice

You can either be in pain and let it consume you,
Or you can use it to fuel you and come out on top.

Taken

So I'm taking it back
I'm letting go of you
And taking everything you took
Leaving you with nothing

Change

People change
"You're different" she mutters
I step back surprised,
thank you.

"You've changed" she says
I smile
thanking her again
for the compliment.

3 years later
I'm looking in the mirror,
I didn't want to be the same
I wanted to grow
and thrive.

People change
but in a relationship,
a healthy one
two must change together.

Different

All this time
I blamed you
for changing
at the flip of a dime.
The subtle changes
the big changes
and everything in-between
that I thought
made us fall.
I thought it was you
changing overnight when really,
it was me
who didn't mean to change at all.

Before/After

Before you
I didn't think I deserved love
I thought what I had
was as good as it got.

Before you
I loved with my whole heart
and expected
the same love back.

Before you
I thought loving someone
would help
and people changed.

After you
I realized
I am worthy of love
for myself and from others.

After you
I loved with my whole heart
but knew
not everyone loves the same.

After you
I realized
some people don't change
no matter how much you love them.

Living Without You

I thought I was happy
the love we shared
that's the way it was
that's the love I knew.

But why did leaving you
give me a breath of fresh air
make me feel alive again
and make me feel true happiness?

All that time
those years
I was lost
thinking I wanted to die.

When in reality
I wanted to live
to be happy
and I had that in me the whole time.

Leaving is the one thing
I can thank you for
the one thing
you did right.

Love shouldn't make you want to die
it shouldn't be all consuming
it shouldn't hurt the way it did
but that's what I learned from loving
myself.

Free

I could breathe again
I had wings on my back
And the world was my oyster
I'm just sorry it had to be this way.

Complete

Humans are funny
we spend our time
searching for another human
to make us happy.

To find that one special person
who 'gets' us
that completes us
and that loves us
like in a fairytale.

we rarely take the time
to love ourselves
expecting someone else
to do a job they can't do themselves.

How can another human
take away your sadness
and your pain
if you can't make yourself happy?

Love isn't completing someone else
it isn't finding someone who tolerates your
flaws
it's finding someone who loves you
after you love yourself.

It's someone who can help you remember
the good in you
who can be there to listen
not someone who stitches you up
or loves every part for you.

True love
is
loving yourself
first.

For Always

Special Thank You:

Cheyenne Raine, for editing and perfecting my words.

: @Rainepublishing

For Always

ABOUT THE AUTHOR

Shannon is a twenty something bisexual self published poet of 8 books and counting. She enjoys coffee, reading, traveling, spending time with her new baby and taking photos.

Check out more work & updates on:

: @Shan_oconnor_

: @Shan_OConnor14

: @Shanoconnor_

Shanoconnor.com

Made in the USA
Monee, IL
19 March 2021